To
_____

From
_____

Date
_____

Experiencing Christ Together Journal
Copyright © 2005 by Brett Eastman
ISBN-10: 0-310-81122-8
ISBN-13: 978-0-310-81122-0

Requests for information should be addressed to:
Inspirio, the gift group of Zondervan
Grand Rapids, Michigan 49530
www.inspiriogifts.com

Printed in China
05 06 07 /CTC/ 4 3 2 1

JOURNAL

EXPERIENCING
CHRIST TOGETHER

xperiencing
CHRIST
together

A Guided Journal by
Brett Eastman

INTRODUCTION

A great spiritual leader once said that the path to true ministry must first start in solitude with God, and effective and lasting ministry for God must come from a quiet place alone with Him. This is why this journal is so important.

The "Greatest Adventure" of our lives will be found in the daily pursuit of knowing, growing, serving, sharing and worshipping Christ forever. The essence of a purposeful life is to see all five biblical purposes fully balanced in our lives. In that balance we will achieve health, which will ultimately lead us to the spiritual growth we all long for as believers. Paul's words to the early church focused on this when he said to "present every man [and woman] complete in Christ" (Colossians 1:28 NASB). In order for any of us to be "complete in Christ," we need to see all five biblical purposes fully formed in our lives.

You and I both know that this doesn't just "magically" happen. It takes a clear sense of purpose, planning, and encouragement from others. This journal is designed to give you and your group an important tool to help in the process of forming Christ deep within your heart and the hearts of your group members.

As he wrote what we know of today as the book of Psalms, David poured out his heart to God. He recorded his honest, most intimate conversations with God in written form. His "journal" included every imaginable emotion, as well as the integration of Old Testament scriptures and simple reflections on every aspect of his life.

I encourage you to carve out a few minutes to pray and plan the first steps in this journal you are about to begin. You can begin by reading the first story in this devotional journal on page 11 and making your first entry on the Day 1 Reflections page. Then decide on which of the approaches listed below with which you want to experiment in reading God's Word and journaling your prayers.

This devotional journal is designed to help you apply the basic habits of reading God's Word and prayer in order for you to cultivate a more intimate walk with Christ. Let me make a few simple suggestions as you begin: As David did, select a source or strategy to help you integrate God's Word into your devotional time. Use any of the following resources:

- Bible
- One Year Bible
- New Testament Bible Challenge Reading Plan
- Devotional Book
- Topical Bible Study Plan

Second, before or after you read God's Word, respond back to God in honest reflection and response to His Word in the form of a written prayer. You may begin this time by simply finishing the sentence: *Father… Yesterday, Lord…* or *Thanks, God, for…* whatever in your life. Share with God where you are in the present moment—express your hurts, disappointments, frustrations, blessings, victories, personal wins, or reasons why you are grateful to God. Whatever you do with your journal, set yourself up to win. You might want to share some of your progress and experiences with some or all of your group members. You may find they want to join in and even encourage you in this journey. Most of all, enjoy the ride and begin to cultivate a more authentic, growing walk with God.

Trust us on this one…This could be one of the greatest adventures of your life.

PERSONAL COVENANT

From this moment on…

I am renewing my commitment to

connect in God's family,

growing to be more like Christ,

develop my gifts for ministry,

share my life mission every day and

surrendering my life for God's pleasure.

———————————————————

Signature

———————————————————

Date

BEGINNING
IN CHRIST TOGETHER

EXPLORING THE PERSON
OF JESUS CHRIST

1

Jesus wasn't someone who made his disciples think, "I want to know what he knows," but someone who made them think, "I want to be like him."

Name one person who has been a hero in your life. What did they do or what qualities did they have that made them heroic to you? In what ways would you like to be like this person?

How does Jesus inspire you to "be like him"?

"The time has come," Jesus said. "The kingdom of God is near. Repent and believe the good news!"

MARK 1:15

Jesus gives you the same invitation he gave his first disciples: Repent. Believe the good news. Follow him. In what specific ways do you need to repent?

In what specific ways do you need to believe the good news?

In what specific ways do you need to follow Jesus?

DAY 1

"Come, follow me," Jesus said, "and I will make you fishers of men."

MARK 1:17

_____

_____

_____

_____

_____

_____

_____

_____

_____

_____

_____

_____

_____

_____

_____

_____

_____

_____

_____

Today's Scripture Passage:

Reflections from my HEART:

I *Honor* who you are. (Praise God for something.)
I *Express* who I'm not. (Confess any known sin.)
I *Affirm* who I am in you. (How does God see you?)
I *Request* your will for me. (Ask God for something.)
I *Thank* you for what you've done. (Thank God for something.)

Today's Action Step:

2

God cares passionately about people, so restoring what is broken in their lives is at the core of his purposes. Jesus' actions say, "These healings are the things the King wants done."

Consider your life at this moment. In what areas of your life (your walk with God, physical health, relationships) do you need the healing touch of Jesus?

"I am willing to heal you." Imagine Jesus saying these words to you. What emotions does this visualization stir inside of you?

Filled with compassion, Jesus reached out his hand and touched the man. "I am willing [to heal you]," he said. "Be clean!"

MARK 1:41

What did Jesus mean when he said, "It is not the healthy who need a doctor, but the sick"? How does this statement make you feel about Jesus?

Who are the "sick" people in your life who need Jesus' healing touch? (List as many as you can.)

In what tangible ways can you share God's love and compassion with each of these people?

> Jesus said to them, "It is not the healthy who need a doctor, but the sick. I have not come to call the righteous, but sinners."
>
> **MARK 2:17**

DAY 2

Today's Scripture Passage:

Reflections from my HEART:

I *Honor* who you are. (Praise God for something.)
I *Express* who I'm not. (Confess any known sin.)
I *Affirm* who I am in you. (How does God see you?)
I *Request* your will for me. (Ask God for something.)
I *Thank* you for what you've done. (Thank God for something.)

DAY
2
_____
_____
_____
_____
_____
_____
_____
_____
_____
_____
_____
_____
_____
_____
_____

Today's Action Step:

_____
_____
_____
_____

3

Your past experiences with care and guidance
(or the lack of them) will affect your relationship
with Jesus the Shepherd.

Think back over your life. Which person (or persons) have provided the most care and guidance to you, especially when you needed it the most?

How can remembering what these people have done for you help you to relate to Jesus as the Good Shepherd.

Jesus said, "I am the good shepherd. The good shepherd lays down his life for the sheep."

JOHN 10:11

How has Jesus proven to be a Good Shepherd for you?
How has he cared for you, protected you, guided you on the right path?

In Jesus' day, sheep were trained to listen to their one, true shepherd's voice;
they knew not to follow the voice of a stranger. In what ways do you need to
hear the Shepherd's voice? What is he speaking to you today?

DAY 3

Jesus said, "My sheep listen to my voice; I know them, and they follow me."

JOHN 10:27

Today's Scripture Passage:

Reflections from my HEART:

I *Honor* who you are. (Praise God for something.)
I *Express* who I'm not. (Confess any known sin.)
I *Affirm* who I am in you. (How does God see you?)
I *Request* your will for me. (Ask God for something.)
I *Thank* you for what you've done. (Thank God for something.)

Today's Action Step:

JOURNAL DAY 4

4

To be a servant was to be a nobody. So when the Son of God took on the "very nature of a servant," he meant to shock the world.

In what ways did Jesus serve others in his lifetime? (List as many as you can think of.)

What areas of service seem to come easy for you? Which areas might be more difficult? Why?

In what ways would having the attitude of a servant begin to transform your life? Which areas need the most of this kind of transformation?

When the time came, Christ Jesus set aside the privileges of deity and took on the status of a slave.

PHILIPPIANS 2:7
THE MESSAGE

How does Jesus' example of service inspire you to serve other people?

List three practical ways in which you can be a servant to another person in the next week.

List some areas of service in which you are currently involved.
What are some areas of service in which you would like to become more active?
What will you do to become more involved in these areas?

Jesus said, "I, your Lord and Teacher, have just washed your feet.
You, then, should wash one another's feet. I have set an example for you,
so that you will do just what I have done for you."
JOHN 13:14–15 TEV

DAY 4

Today's Scripture Passage:

Reflections from my HEART:

I *Honor* who you are. (Praise God for something.)

I *Express* who I'm not. (Confess any known sin.)

I *Affirm* who I am in you. (How does God see you?)

I *Request* your will for me. (Ask God for something.)

I *Thank* you for what you've done. (Thank God for something.)

DAY

4

Today's Action Step:

Jesus deliberately took our sin upon himself. In his final moments, he declared that he had paid the full price of our debt and accomplished his mission on earth.

Not only did Jesus come to redeem the entire world, but he also came to save you personally. In what ways has Jesus saved you in the past?

From what things do you need saving today?

The man Christ Jesus gave himself to redeem all mankind. That was the proof that God wants everyone to be saved,

1 TIMOTHY 2:5–6 TEV

Jesus had you in mind when he went to the cross.
How does thinking of this affect how God views you when you sin?

How have you recently responded to Jesus the Savior?

How has Jesus' death changed the way that you live?

DAY 5

We are made right in God's sight when we trust in Jesus Christ to take away our sins. And we all can be saved in this same way, no matter who we are or what we have done.
ROMANS 3:22 NLT

Today's Scripture Passage:

Reflections from my HEART:

I *Honor* who you are. (Praise God for something.)
I *Express* who I'm not. (Confess any known sin.)
I *Affirm* who I am in you. (How does God see you?)
I *Request* your will for me. (Ask God for something.)
I *Thank* you for what you've done. (Thank God for something.)

_____
_____
_____
_____
_____
_____
_____
_____
_____
_____
_____
_____
_____
_____
_____
_____

Today's Action Step:

_____
_____
_____
_____

6

The resurrection isn't just a Hollywood ending to a nice story. It's an invitation for us to start fresh, to take Christ's promise of new life seriously.

What does the fact that Jesus rose from the dead mean to you? How has it affected your life?

After Jesus rose from the dead, Mary Magdalene saw him but did not recognize him—until he said her name. (See John 20:10–18.) How has the Risen Lord "spoken your name" recently? How has this experience caused you to see him more clearly?

Jesus Christ our Lord was shown to be the Son of God when God powerfully raised him from the dead by means of the Holy Spirit.

ROMANS 1:4 NLT

Jesus' resurrection demonstrated his power over sin and death.
In what ways do you need this power to become effective in your life?

True surrender means giving up doing life your own way and, instead,
doing life God's way with everything you've got. Which area or person in your
life do you most need to surrender to the Risen Lord? Write a prayer of surrender,
giving him complete control and allowing him to bring his resurrection power
into the situation.

> What we believe is this: If we get included in Christ's sin-conquering death,
> we also get included in his life-saving resurrection.
>
> **ROMANS 6:8 THE MESSAGE**

DAY
6

Today's Scripture Passage:

Reflections from my HEART:

I *Honor* who you are. (Praise God for something.)

I *Express* who I'm not. (Confess any known sin.)

I *Affirm* who I am in you. (How does God see you?)

I *Request* your will for me. (Ask God for something.)

I *Thank* you for what you've done. (Thank God for something.)

DAY

6

_____

_____

_____

_____

_____

_____

_____

_____

_____

_____

_____

_____

_____

_____

_____

_____

Today's Action Step:

_____

_____

_____

_____

As I grow in the Lord by reading his Word,
what am I learning from the life of Christ
(his identity, his personality, his priorities)?

How does he want me to live differently?

CONNECTING IN CHRIST TOGETHER

FELLOWSHIP

Love is the ultimate test of whether you have
Christ in you or not.

In what ways has your life been a reflection of Christ's love?

In what ways have other people in your life reflected Christ's love back to you?

The more you "remain," or "abide," in Jesus' love for you, the more you'll love
others. List some specific ways in which you can "abide" in Jesus.

Jesus said, "As the
Father has loved me,
so have I loved you.
Now remain in my
love."

JOHN 15:9

Who is one person in your life that especially needs to experience love?
How can you lay your life down for them, in order to be a reflection of Christ's love?

Who is one person in your life that is especially difficult to love?
How can you practice the sacrificial love of Jesus toward that person?

Describe the difference that Christ's love has made in your life.

DAY 7

Jesus said, "My command is this: Love each other as I have loved you. Greater love has no one than this, that he lay down his life for his friends."

JOHN 15:12–13

Today's Scripture Passage:

Reflections from my HEART:

I *Honor* who you are. (Praise God for something.)
I *Express* who I'm not. (Confess any known sin.)
I *Affirm* who I am in you. (How does God see you?)
I *Request* your will for me. (Ask God for something.)
I *Thank* you for what you've done. (Thank God for something.)

_____
_____
_____
_____
_____
_____
_____
_____
_____
_____
_____
_____
_____
_____
_____
_____

Today's Action Step:

_____
_____
_____
_____

8

Jesus demonstrated what it looks like to love sacrificially, even shocking his disciples that he was willing to take love for his friends so far.

When Jesus' friend Lazarus died, Jesus responded, despite the personal cost and the danger it put him in. How does his example inspire you to love others?

Has anyone ever loved you sacrificially—given up something important to care for you in some way? How did you feel when you realized what they'd done?

Jesus wept.
Then the Jews said,
"See how he loved him!"

JOHN 11:35–36

In Philippians 2:20-21 Paul spoke of Timothy: "I have no one else like him, who takes a genuine interest in your welfare. For everyone looks out for his own interests, not those of Jesus Christ". Describe the connection between taking an interest in the welfare of others and looking out for the interests of Jesus.

Name someone who needs your sacrificial love. What can you do to "look out for the interests of Jesus" in this situation?

List five tangible ways you can express the sacrificial love of Christ in the next week.

In the process of finishing up that work,
Epaphroditus put his life on the line and nearly died doing it.

PHILIPPIANS 2:30 THE MESSAGE

DAY
8

Today's Scripture Passage:

Reflections from my HEART:

I *Honor* who you are. (Praise God for something.)
I *Express* who I'm not. (Confess any known sin.)
I *Affirm* who I am in you. (How does God see you?)
I *Request* your will for me. (Ask God for something.)
I *Thank* you for what you've done. (Thank God for something.)

DAY
8

Today's Action Step:

9

Loving sinners is messy.
But because we're in the family of God together,
we need to learn how to love as Jesus loved.

What does it mean to you to "hate the sin, but love the sinner"?

Have you ever known someone who habitually sinned, but continually asked for forgiveness? How did you feel toward that person? How do you think Jesus feels toward them?

> God did not send his
> Son into the world to
> condemn the world,
> but to save the world
> through him.
>
> **JOHN 3:17**

How has God loved you despite your sin? Describe some of your most recent sins, and express gratitude for his forgiveness. Thank him for the chance to try again with his help. Imagine Jesus looking at you with love and understanding. He knows everything you've done, and why. He doesn't condone your faults, but he offers you forgiveness and a chance to become who you were meant to be.

DAY 9

"Neither do I condemn you," Jesus declared.
"Go now and leave your life of sin."

JOHN 8:11

Today's Scripture Passage:

Reflections from my HEART:

I *Honor* who you are. (Praise God for something.)
I *Express* who I'm not. (Confess any known sin.)
I *Affirm* who I am in you. (How does God see you?)
I *Request* your will for me. (Ask God for something.)
I *Thank* you for what you've done. (Thank God for something.)

_____

_____

_____

_____

_____

_____

_____

_____

_____

_____

_____

_____

_____

_____

_____

Today's Action Step:

_____

_____

_____

10

Jesus didn't just tell people what they wanted to hear. He told them what they needed to hear.

When confronting other people, do you tend to be more "tough" or more "tender"? How does this compare to Jesus' balanced approach?

Have you ever been confronted by someone in a "tough" way? In a "tender" way? How did you respond in each instance? Why did you respond this way?

By speaking the truth in a spirit of love, we must grow up in every way.

EPHESIANS 4:15 TEV

Are there times when more "tenderness" than "toughness" is called for? What about vice versa? How can you know in which attitude to proceed?

Is there someone whom you need to confront? If so, list three specific, practical ways in which you can approach them with gentleness and humility.

Dear brothers, if a Christian is overcome by some sin, you who are godly should gently and humbly help him back onto the right path, remembering that next time it might be one of you who is in the wrong.

GALATIANS 6:1 TLB

DAY
10

Today's Scripture Passage:

Reflections from my HEART:

I *Honor* who you are. (Praise God for something.)
I *Express* who I'm not. (Confess any known sin.)
I *Affirm* who I am in you. (How does God see you?)
I *Request* your will for me. (Ask God for something.)
I *Thank* you for what you've done. (Thank God for something.)

DAY
10

_____
_____
_____
_____
_____
_____
_____
_____
_____
_____
_____
_____
_____
_____
_____
_____
_____
_____

Today's Action Step:

_____
_____
_____
_____

Nothing in Jesus' teachings seems more outrageous than his ideas about forgiveness and loving enemies.

11

What does the phrase "turning the other cheek" mean to you, in a practical sense? Is it possible to take this concept too far?

How do you react to Jesus' instruction to "love your enemies"? With anger? With dread? With fear for what it will cost you? What would it take for you to respond with joy?

Jesus said, "Love your enemies, do good to those who hate you, bless those who curse you, pray for those who mistreat you."

LUKE 6:27–28

Think of someone who has hurt you, or whom you consider an "enemy."
What can you do to begin to treat that person with love?

Think of someone who has recently taken advantage of you.
How does Jesus want you to respond to their behavior?

What are three practical ways in which you will "love your enemy" this week?

DAY 11

Jesus said, "If someone grabs your shirt, giftwrap your best coat and make a present of it.... Love your enemies. You'll never—I promise—regret it."

LUKE 6:29, 35 THE MESSAGE

experiencing
CHRIST
together

Today's Scripture Passage:

Reflections from my HEART:

I *Honor* who you are. (Praise God for something.)
I *Express* who I'm not. (Confess any known sin.)
I *Affirm* who I am in you. (How does God see you?)
I *Request* your will for me. (Ask God for something.)
I *Thank* you for what you've done. (Thank God for something.)

_____

_____

_____

_____

_____

_____

_____

_____

_____

_____

_____

_____

_____

_____

_____

_____

_____

Today's Action Step:

_____

_____

_____

12

The harder we look at the cross,
making it the lens through which we see life,
the more Jesus' command to "love one another"
will become our natural response.

What specific things has Jesus done that demonstrate his love for you?
In what ways have these acts of love motivated you to love other people?

Sometimes it's easy to forget what Jesus suffered on the cross—all because
of his love for us. How can you remind yourself more frequently of his sacrifice—
and his example?

We know what real love
is because Christ gave up
his life for us. And so we
also ought to give up our
lives for our Christian
brothers and sisters.

1 JOHN 3:16 NLT

Jesus died to cleanse us from our sins, especially our failure to love God and others as we should. This love includes:

- Laying down your life for another person
- Showing up and taking action
- Treating a sinful person with warmth instead of condemnation
- Telling someone a hard truth with a tender heart
- Forgiving someone who harms you

Write the name of a person or persons whom you have recently failed to love in one of these ways. What can you do in the next week to begin to show Jesus' love to them?

Write a prayer to God, asking for forgiveness for your failure to love as Jesus loved you, and for help in following through with your commitment to try again.

DAY
12

Your attitude should be the same as that of Christ Jesus: ... He humbled himself and became obedient to death—even death on a cross!

PHILIPPIANS 2:5, 8

experiencing
CHRIST
together

Today's Scripture Passage:

Reflections from my HEART:

I *Honor* who you are. (Praise God for something.)
I *Express* who I'm not. (Confess any known sin.)
I *Affirm* who I am in you. (How does God see you?)
I *Request* your will for me. (Ask God for something.)
I *Thank* you for what you've done. (Thank God for something.)

DAY
12

_____

Today's Action Step:

As I grow in the Lord by reading his Word, what am I learning from the life of Christ (his identity, his personality, his priorities)?

12

How does he want me to live differently?

GROWING IN CHRIST TOGETHER

DISCIPLESHIP

Christ loves you the way you are.
But he also has a vision for who you can become.

What areas of your life are the hardest to surrender to Christ? Why?

What personal costs have you paid in order to follow Christ?
Were they "worth it" to you? Why or why not?

Jesus said, "Anyone
who intends to come
with me has to let me
lead. You're not in the
driver's seat—I am."

LUKE 9:23
THE MESSAGE

Consider Jesus' statement, "Whoever loses his life for me will save it." What does it mean to "lose your life" for him? How will your life be "saved" in return?

What "costs" have you paid in your own life for not following Christ? Which have been the hardest to pay?

What rewards have you gained from following him?

DAY 13

Jesus said, "Whoever wants to save his life will lose it, but whoever loses his life for me will save it."

LUKE 9:24

Today's Scripture Passage:

Reflections from my HEART:

I *Honor* who you are. (Praise God for something.)
I *Express* who I'm not. (Confess any known sin.)
I *Affirm* who I am in you. (How does God see you?)
I *Request* your will for me. (Ask God for something.)
I *Thank* you for what you've done. (Thank God for something.)

DAY 13

_____
_____
_____
_____
_____
_____
_____
_____
_____
_____
_____
_____
_____
_____
_____
_____

Today's Action Step:

_____
_____
_____

14

God sometimes empties and dries us out so he can fill us with his life. During times of emptiness, we become most dependent on God.

Have you ever been "led by the Spirit" into a "desert experience"? Explain.

Was God able to turn this hard time into something good, to be used for his glory? If so, how did he accomplish this?

Jesus was led by the Spirit in the desert, where for forty days he was tempted by the devil.

LUKE 4:1–2

Satan loves to try to sabotage the desert experiences that God wants to turn for our good. Has he ever tempted you in a vulnerable time of your life? How did you respond?

During past desert experiences, how has God helped you through (i.e., his Word, other believers, prayer)?

How do your past experiences in the desert help you to face current or future difficult times?

> The LORD said: "I remember the devotion of your youth,
> how as a bride you loved me and followed me through the desert."
>
> **JEREMIAH 2:2**

DAY 14

_____

_____

_____

_____

_____

_____

_____

_____

_____

_____

_____

_____

_____

_____

_____

_____

_____

_____

experiencing
CHRIST
together

14

Can you relate in any way to the temptations of Jesus?

"If you are the Son of God, turn these stones into bread" (see Luke 4:3). Jesus was hungry. The devil asked him to fulfill his physical needs in an inappropriate way. Can you relate to this temptation? If so, how?

"If you bow down and worship me, I will give you the kingdoms of the world" (see Luke 4:7). Jesus was the true and rightful King, but Satan offered him the "fast track" to what was already his. Have you ever been tempted to forcefully take something that rightfully belonged to you? Have you ever been tempted to act on a promise of God—but out of his timing?

"If you are the Son of God, throw yourself off the pinnacle of the temple, and the angels will catch you" (see Luke 4:9–10). Have you ever been tempted with the desire of fame? How about looking good in front of— or even more righteous than—other people?

Jesus was able to stand strong against the temptations of Satan because he had spent time fasting and he was full of God's Word. List some ways that you can prepare ahead of time for whatever temptations the devil might bring into your life.

DAY
14

Today's Scripture Passage:

Reflections from my HEART:

I *Honor* who you are. (Praise God for something.)

I *Express* who I'm not. (Confess any known sin.)

I *Affirm* who I am in you. (How does God see you?)

I *Request* your will for me. (Ask God for something.)

I *Thank* you for what you've done. (Thank God for something.)

DAY

14

Today's Action Step:

Hurry is a disease in our culture.
But your number-one priority should be:
Love God with everything you've got and
love others as yourself.

15

Is it typically easy or difficult for you to take time out of your schedule and spend it in solitude and prayer? Why or why not?

What changes would you see in your life if you were able to spend more quiet time with God? Are these changes worth the sacrifice that it might take to do so? Why or why not?

"Step out of the traffic! Take a long, loving look at me, your High God."

PSALM 46:10
THE MESSAGE

In what situations do you most need the quiet solitude and peace of God? What can you do to take a step back and experience his rest?

Write a prayer of commitment to the Lord, to begin or maintain a personal quiet time alone with him. Describe for him why you enjoy spending time with him.

DAY 15

The LORD is my shepherd, I shall not be in want.
He makes me lie down in green pastures,
he leads me beside quiet waters, he restores my soul.

PSALM 23:1–3

TIPS FOR A FRUITFUL
PERSONAL TIME WITH GOD

1. Set a definite time—a time when you will be most alert.

2. Choose a quiet place—a place where you won't be disturbed.

3. Start out with just ten or fifteen minutes.

4. Include Bible reading, prayer, and confession of any sin you're aware of.

5. Be habitual about it; it takes about six weeks to develop a new habit.

6. Determine ahead of time what you are going to do.

7. Be creative; consider varying the things you do during your quiet time (Bible reading, listening to a worship CD, journaling your praise to God, meditating on a single verse or passage of Scripture).

8. Write down in your journal what you are learning about God and what you believe he wants you to do (submit to correction, respond in a specific act of obedience, offer him praise, accept his forgiveness, bow before him in repentance).

Today's Scripture Passage:

Reflections from my HEART:

I *Honor* who you are. (Praise God for something.)
I *Express* who I'm not. (Confess any known sin.)
I *Affirm* who I am in you. (How does God see you?)
I *Request* your will for me. (Ask God for something.)
I *Thank* you for what you've done. (Thank God for something.)

DAY

15

Today's Action Step:

16

Jesus wanted his disciples to pray from hearts of love
to a Father who loved them.

What past experiences have helped or hindered you in viewing God
as a loving Father?

What are some challenges you are currently facing in your prayer life?
What are some practical ways you can overcome these challenges?

Jesus said to them,
"In this manner,
therefore, pray:
Our Father in
heaven. Hallowed
be Your name."

MATTHEW 6:9 NKJV

Take some time out of your busy schedule and spend a half an hour with God in prayer. On this page, write a letter to God, expressing whatever is on your heart.

DAY 16

Do not be anxious about anything, but in everything, by prayer and petition, with thanksgiving, present your requests to God.

PHILIPPIANS 4:6

Today's Scripture Passage:

Reflections from my HEART:

I *Honor* who you are. (Praise God for something.)
I *Express* who I'm not. (Confess any known sin.)
I *Affirm* who I am in you. (How does God see you?)
I *Request* your will for me. (Ask God for something.)
I *Thank* you for what you've done. (Thank God for something.)

_____
_____
_____
_____
_____
_____
_____
_____
_____
_____
_____
_____
_____
_____

Today's Action Step:

_____
_____
_____

17

We need to be like Christ in his quiet moments
and in his active obedience to his Father.
For Jesus, deep obedience came naturally
because he knew his Father's love.

Unless we trust God to have our best interests at heart, we will obey him fearfully,
if at all. What motivates you to obey God—fear, or his love for you? Why?

Jesus said that the wise person puts his words into practice habitually, before
a storm hits. How do you make obedience a habit in the "calm" times?
When has this helped to see you through a more difficult time in your life?

Jesus said, "A good
man out of the good
treasure of his heart
brings forth good."

LUKE 6:45 NKJV

How does your obedience to what Jesus has told you to do demonstrate the quality of your own faith?

In what areas is Jesus asking you for your obedience?
What can you do to surrender those areas over to his control?

Jesus asked, "Why do you call me, 'Lord, Lord,' and do not do what I say? ...
[he who] hears my words and puts them into practice ... is like a man
building a house, who ... laid the foundation on rock."
LUKE 6:46–48

DAY
17

Today's Scripture Passage:

Reflections from my HEART:

I *Honor* who you are. (Praise God for something.)
I *Express* who I'm not. (Confess any known sin.)
I *Affirm* who I am in you. (How does God see you?)
I *Request* your will for me. (Ask God for something.)
I *Thank* you for what you've done. (Thank God for something.)

DAY

17

Today's Action Step:

Whether we're packrats, big spenders, or living lean, we all need to think about what we treasure and why.

18

Do you tend to be more "frugal" or more "frivolous" in your spending habits? Why?

What "treasures in heaven" have you recently "stored up"?

Jesus said, "Store up for yourselves treasures in heaven, where moth and rust do not destroy, and where thieves do not break in and steal."

MATTHEW 6:20

What day-to-day needs concern you today? Write a prayer to your heavenly Father, asking him to meet your needs as you place his kingdom first in your life.

In what practical ways can you put God's kingdom first in the upcoming week?

DAY
18

Your heavenly Father ... will give you all you need from day to day if you live for him and make the Kingdom of God your primary concern.

MATTHEW 6:32–33 NLT

Today's Scripture Passage:

Reflections from my HEART:

I *Honor* who you are. (Praise God for something.)
I *Express* who I'm not. (Confess any known sin.)
I *Affirm* who I am in you. (How does God see you?)
I *Request* your will for me. (Ask God for something.)
I *Thank* you for what you've done. (Thank God for something.)

DAY 18

_____
_____
_____
_____
_____
_____
_____
_____
_____
_____
_____
_____
_____
_____
_____
_____
_____

Today's Action Step:

_____
_____
_____
_____

18

As I grow in the Lord by reading his Word, what am I learning from the life of Christ (his identity, his personality, his priorities)?

How does he want me to live differently?

SERVING LIKE CHRIST TOGETHER

MINISTRY

Service is often unglamorous.
But for those who desire to follow Christ,
no act of service is beneath them,
because they've acquired Jesus' servant heart.

19

When you think of the word success, what sort of ideas usually come to your mind?
How are these ideas similar to or different from Jesus' definition of success?

What would it look like for you to be successful in Jesus' eyes?

Jesus said, "If one of
you wants to be great,
he must be the servant
of the rest; and if one
of you wants to be first,
he must be the slave
of all."

MARK 10:43–44 TEV

Have you ever tried to honor yourself, but ended up being humbled?
Or have you humbled yourself, but ultimately were honored?
Describe the situation.

In what current situation of your life do you need to practice servanthood
and humility?

DAY
19

Jesus said, "Everyone who tries to honor himself shall be humbled;
and he who humbles himself shall be honored."

LUKE 14:11 TLB

Today's Scripture Passage:

Reflections from my HEART:

I *Honor* who you are. (Praise God for something.)
I *Express* who I'm not. (Confess any known sin.)
I *Affirm* who I am in you. (How does God see you?)
I *Request* your will for me. (Ask God for something.)
I *Thank* you for what you've done. (Thank God for something.)

DAY 19

_____
_____
_____
_____
_____
_____
_____
_____
_____
_____
_____
_____
_____
_____
_____
_____
_____

Today's Action Step:

_____
_____
_____
_____

20

Faith and action go hand in hand.
Our service flows out of our commitment to Christ.

If someone were to determine your level of faith strictly based on your outward actions, what would be their conclusion? Why?

What actions is God currently pressing on your heart to do?
What will it take for you to be obedient?

"Show me how anyone
can have faith without
actions. I will show you
my faith by my actions."

JAMES 2:18 TEV

How difficult or easy is it for you to "back up" your faith with action?

What are the obstacles that stand in the way of your combining your beliefs with your behavior?

Write a prayer asking for God's help to overcome these obstacles and his strength to put your faith into action this week.

> Faith without works is dead.
>
> **JAMES 2:26 NASB**

DAY
20

_____

_____

_____

_____

_____

_____

_____

_____

_____

_____

_____

_____

_____

_____

_____

_____

_____

_____

experiencing
CHRIST
together

Today's Scripture Passage:

Reflections from my HEART:

I *Honor* who you are. (Praise God for something.)
I *Express* who I'm not. (Confess any known sin.)
I *Affirm* who I am in you. (How does God see you?)
I *Request* your will for me. (Ask God for something.)
I *Thank* you for what you've done. (Thank God for something.)

DAY

20

_____

_____

_____

_____

_____

_____

_____

_____

_____

_____

_____

_____

_____

_____

_____

Today's Action Step:

_____

_____

_____

_____

21

Compassion is the ability to feel or see another person's need—along with the decision to address that need through action.

Have you ever been lost, like a "sheep without a shepherd"? How has Jesus had compassion on you during those times?

How did Jesus' compassion make you feel? What changes did it prompt in your life?

When Jesus landed and saw a large crowd, he had compassion on them, because they were like sheep without a shepherd.

MARK 6:34

Who are the sheep without shepherds around you?
What about them or their lives causes you to consider them in this way?

What can you do to demonstrate Jesus' compassion—love in action—
to these people? Be specific.

DAY 21

Finally, all of you be of one mind, having compassion for one another;
love as brothers, be tenderhearted.

1 PETER 3:8 NKJV

Today's Scripture Passage:

Reflections from my HEART:

I *Honor* who you are. (Praise God for something.)
I *Express* who I'm not. (Confess any known sin.)
I *Affirm* who I am in you. (How does God see you?)
I *Request* your will for me. (Ask God for something.)
I *Thank* you for what you've done. (Thank God for something.)

Today's Action Step:

22

Without the Holy Spirit, none of us can serve as Jesus served. The Spirit is the power in a servant's heart.

Have you ever experienced the Holy Spirit strengthening, guiding, and helping you as you serve other people? If so, describe the experience.

What things in your life might be preventing the Holy Spirit from fully flowing through you? What could you do to allow him to work through you in a greater way?

Jesus said, "I will ask the Father, and he will give you another Counselor to be with you forever."

JOHN 14:16

What is one current area in your life in which you need the guidance and strength of the Holy Spirit?

How could the "rivers of living water" change the situation?

Jesus said, "Rivers of living water will brim and spill out of the depths of anyone who believes in me." (He said this in regard to the Spirit, whom those who believed in him were about to receive.)
JOHN 7:38–39 THE MESSAGE

_____
_____
_____
_____
_____
_____
_____
_____
_____
_____
_____
_____
_____
_____
_____
_____
_____
_____

JOURNAL DAY 22

22

The Holy Spirit longs to guide us in many areas—to know Christ more intimately, to love him more deeply, to serve him more fully. However, when we seek wisdom from our Counselor, we are often most interested in guidance that will make our own lives easier or more pleasant: "If I take this job, will it lead to financial success?" "Which potential marriage partner will make me the most happy?" The Holy Spirit is generally more focused on God's agenda. He wants us to ask questions such as, "Where is God at work around me?" and, "How can I contribute?" Prayerfully consider these questions, and then ask the Lord, "How can I serve you?" Record his response below.

Lord, how can I serve you?

Today's Scripture Passage:

Reflections from my HEART:

I *Honor* who you are. (Praise God for something.)
I *Express* who I'm not. (Confess any known sin.)
I *Affirm* who I am in you. (How does God see you?)
I *Request* your will for me. (Ask God for something.)
I *Thank* you for what you've done. (Thank God for something.)

Today's Action Step:

23

It may naturally offend us to think of Jesus asking us to take on the attitude of a slave. Unfortunately, he does exactly that.

How much do you consider yourself a "slave" of God—that he has bought you and that you don't belong to yourself?

God asks us to place his agenda above our own. Do you trust that he has your best interests at heart? Why or why not?

Jesus said, "When you obey me you should say, 'We are not worthy of praise. We are servants who have simply done our duty.'"

LUKE 17:10 NLT

In most groups, families, or workplaces, there are usually some persons who think of their duties ahead of their rights—who defer to others, who listen, who serve. There are also those who think of their rights ahead of their duties—who strive to get their own way, who are happy to let others carry the heaviest load, and who may even take advantage of others.

How do you usually relate to members of the first group? To members of the second group? How would Jesus relate to these people?

Into which group do you fall? Explain your answer.

What can you do to ensure that you consistently belong to the first group? Write a prayer asking God to help you consistently think of others before yourself.

DAY 23

All your lives you've let sin tell you what to do. But thank God you've started listening to a new master, one whose commands set you free to live openly in his freedom!

ROMANS 6:16–18
THE MESSAGE

experiencing
CHRIST
together

Today's Scripture Passage:

Reflections from my HEART:

I *Honor* who you are. (Praise God for something.)
I *Express* who I'm not. (Confess any known sin.)
I *Affirm* who I am in you. (How does God see you?)
I *Request* your will for me. (Ask God for something.)
I *Thank* you for what you've done. (Thank God for something.)

DAY
23

Today's Action Step:

24

Most of us have an unwritten list of people
we'd prefer not to serve.
Jesus invites us to widen our circle of service
to include those on our unwritten list.

Who are the people on your "unwritten list"? Why is it so difficult for you to serve these people?

In what ways do you think God might bless you for your hospitality to these particular people?

Jesus said, "When you give a banquet, invite the poor, the crippled, the lame, the blind, and you will be blessed."

LUKE 14:13–14

Has there ever been a time when you offered service or hospitality, but you did so with a poor attitude? How do you think God felt about your service at that time?

How, in a practical sense, can you begin to practice hospitality and serve others with the attitude of Christ? What holds you back? What can you do about these obstacles?

Write a prayer of surrender to God, asking him to help you serve your "unwritten list" of people, as well as anyone else he sends to you, with the attitude of Jesus.

DAY 24

Offer hospitality to one another without grumbling.

1 PETER 4:9

Today's Scripture Passage:

Reflections from my HEART:

I *Honor* who you are. (Praise God for something.)
I *Express* who I'm not. (Confess any known sin.)
I *Affirm* who I am in you. (How does God see you?)
I *Request* your will for me. (Ask God for something.)
I *Thank* you for what you've done. (Thank God for something.)

_____
_____
_____
_____
_____
_____
_____
_____
_____
_____
_____
_____
_____
_____
_____
_____

Today's Action Step:

_____
_____
_____

24

As I grow in the Lord by reading his Word,
what am I learning from the life of Christ
(his identity, his personality, his priorities)?

How does he want me to live differently?

SHARING CHRIST
TOGETHER

EVANGELISM

God wants evangelism to well up from within us
because our hearts are taking on the character of Jesus.

25

How strong was Jesus' passion for the lost in his lifetime on earth?
How strong is it today?

How strong is your own passion for the lost? Explain. What can you do to
foster in your own heart a Christ-like attitude toward a lost and dying world?

Jesus said, "Heaven
will be happier over one
lost sinner who returns
to God than over ninety-
nine others who are
righteous and haven't
strayed away!"

LUKE 15:7 NLT

Do you remember a time when you were a "lost sheep"?
How did Jesus help you find your way home?

Who are the "lost sheep" in your life—people who yet need to have an
encounter with Christ? List the people God lays on your heart in each of
the following areas, and then write a prayer, asking God to help you share
his love with them in the next few weeks.

DAY 25

GOD says, "My people were lost sheep....
They lost track of home, couldn't remember where they came from."

JEREMIAH 50:6 THE MESSAGE

_____
_____
_____
_____
_____
_____
_____
_____
_____
_____
_____
_____
_____
_____
_____
_____
_____
_____
_____

Family members (immediate or extended):

Friends:

Acquaintances (neighbors, kids' sports teams, school, and so forth):

Work colleagues:

People you meet just for fun (gym, hobbies, hangouts):

_____

_____

_____

_____

_____

_____

_____

_____

_____

_____

_____

_____

_____

_____

_____

_____

_____

_____

_____

_____

_____

_____

Today's Scripture Passage:

Reflections from my HEART:

I *Honor* who you are. (Praise God for something.)
I *Express* who I'm not. (Confess any known sin.)
I *Affirm* who I am in you. (How does God see you?)
I *Request* your will for me. (Ask God for something.)
I *Thank* you for what you've done. (Thank God for something.)

DAY
25

_____

Today's Action Step:

26

When God wanted to offer his love to a lost world,
he came in the flesh.
He is still present in the flesh in people like you.

Have you ever been Christ's "in-the-flesh" presence to an unbeliever?
What did you do?

In what ways might Jesus be asking you to be his hands, his feet,
his voice to the people around you who need to know him? Be specific.

The Word became
flesh and made his
dwelling among us.

JOHN 1:14

Jesus came to "seek out" the lost. How active are you in seeking out those people who do not yet have a relationship with God?

In what ways could you be more active? What is holding you back?

List three specific ways in which you can "seek out the lost" and be Christ's "in-the-flesh" presence to them this week.

DAY 26

Jesus said, "The Son of Man came to seek and to save what was lost."

LUKE 19:10

Today's Scripture Passage:

Reflections from my HEART:

I *Honor* who you are. (Praise God for something.)
I *Express* who I'm not. (Confess any known sin.)
I *Affirm* who I am in you. (How does God see you?)
I *Request* your will for me. (Ask God for something.)
I *Thank* you for what you've done. (Thank God for something.)

DAY 26

Today's Action Step:

THE SKILL OF
LISTENING FOR NEEDS

READ JOHN 4:4–29.

With insight from the Holy Spirit, Jesus knew that the Samaritan woman had five husbands. The Holy Spirit may not give you such dramatic insight about strangers, but he does desire to help you discern the felt needs and real needs of people around you. You can learn to notice the broken places in people's lives. Sensitive questions and practical acts, such as giving and receiving water, can speak powerfully to people about your respect and concern for them. Most people are as thirsty for respect and kindness as the Samaritan woman was.

Jesus modeled how to discern a person's real needs. As you listen to the needs someone expresses, you can simply ask a few caring questions that invite her to share more of her heart with you. By listening well, you can draw her out further.

The Five R's of Listening help to keep a conversation going and create an atmosphere that draws someone out:

1. Repeat what the person has shared with you.
2. Repeat his last sentence to encourage him to share more.
3. Return his comment with another question.
4. Respond with affirmation and gratitude for his willingness to share.
5. Renew your commitment to listen and pray for him.

In the next few days, practice using these Five R's in conversation with the people around you. Then record your responses to the following questions.

Did the use of the Five R's enhance your conversation(s) in any way? If so, how?

What did you learn from these conversation(s)?

What will you do differently the next time?

DAY 26

27

One of the most important ways we can sow seeds of the gospel in a person's life is to discuss common human experiences. These conversations are seeds, and it's God's job to make them grow.

Who are some of the unbelievers you encounter on a regular basis? What types of conversations can you begin to have with these people in order to become a witness to them?

Have you ever presented the gospel to someone who ultimately declined? How did you react? How would viewing that experience as a "seed-planting opportunity" have changed your reaction?

Whatever a person is like, I try to find common ground with him so that he will let me tell him about Christ and let Christ save him. I do this to get the Gospel to them and also for the blessing I myself receive when I see them come to Christ.

1 CORINTHIANS 9:22–23
TLB

Have you ever presented the gospel to someone who accepted? How did you feel? How did God bless you as a result?

How can you go about building stronger relationships with non-believers? List some practical ways you can do this in the next week.

> We are Christ's ... ambassadors, as though God were making his appeal through us. We implore you on Christ's behalf: Be reconciled to God.
>
> **2 CORINTHIANS 5:20**

DAY

27

_____

_____

_____

_____

_____

_____

_____

_____

_____

_____

_____

_____

_____

_____

_____

_____

_____

_____

Today's Scripture Passage:

Reflections from my HEART:

I *Honor* who you are. (Praise God for something.)
I *Express* who I'm not. (Confess any known sin.)
I *Affirm* who I am in you. (How does God see you?)
I *Request* your will for me. (Ask God for something.)
I *Thank* you for what you've done. (Thank God for something.)

DAY
27

Today's Action Step:

28

Socializing and communicating
across a cultural divide takes work.
Yet Jesus encourages us to widen our view
and notice needs among persons
who may be very different from us.

Have you ever witnessed of Christ's love to someone from another culture?
Why or why not?

Which ethnic groups do you find the most difficult to relate to?
Which are the easiest? Explain your answer.

God was reconciling
the world to himself
in Christ.

2 CORINTHIANS 5:19

What opportunities do you personally have to minister to the physical or spiritual needs of people from other cultures, both at home and in other countries?

How have you taken advantage of these opportunities? If you have not taken advantage of them, why not?

How would you handle an opportunity to speak about your faith to someone from a different culture? What are some of the things you would say?

<table>
<tr><td>DAY
28</td><td>Pray for us, that God may open a door for our message,
so that we may proclaim the mystery of Christ.
COLOSSIANS 4:3</td></tr>
</table>

_____

_____

_____

_____

_____

_____

_____

_____

_____

_____

_____

_____

_____

_____

_____

_____

_____

_____

experiencing
CHRIST
together

Today's Scripture Passage:

Reflections from my HEART:

I *Honor* who you are. (Praise God for something.)
I *Express* who I'm not. (Confess any known sin.)
I *Affirm* who I am in you. (How does God see you?)
I *Request* your will for me. (Ask God for something.)
I *Thank* you for what you've done. (Thank God for something.)

_____

_____

_____

_____

_____

_____

_____

_____

_____

_____

_____

_____

_____

_____

_____

Today's Action Step:

_____

_____

_____

29

Jesus never intended most of his disciples
to be solo evangelists.
He expected them to make it as a team.

Does the idea of working as a team to spread the gospel encourage you or cause
you to feel hindered? What are the advantages to working together?

What are the disadvantages?

The Lord appointed
seventy-two others and
sent them two by two
ahead of him to every
town and place where
he was about to go.

LUKE 10:1

What risks does teamwork in evangelism alleviate? What risks are you willing to take for your faith? Which risks might be considered foolish if they could be avoided?

Name several people in your life with whom you could "team up" to share the gospel in a certain place or setting. How might you approach them to coordinate such an effort?

Jesus prayed, "May [my disciples] be brought to complete unity to let the world know that you sent me and have loved them even as you have loved me."

JOHN 17:23

DAY
29

_____
_____
_____
_____
_____
_____
_____
_____
_____
_____
_____
_____
_____
_____
_____
_____
_____
_____
_____

Today's Scripture Passage:

Reflections from my HEART:

I *Honor* who you are. (Praise God for something.)
I *Express* who I'm not. (Confess any known sin.)
I *Affirm* who I am in you. (How does God see you?)
I *Request* your will for me. (Ask God for something.)
I *Thank* you for what you've done. (Thank God for something.)

DAY
29

Today's Action Step:

It's tempting to avert our eyes
when we see signs of people's brokenness.
But Jesus singled out the messed up, the immoral,
the people who were in trouble and needed help.

Jesus made "sick" people a priority in his life over "healthy" people.
Is this priority reflected in your own life? Why or why not?

It is important to keep a balance between spending time with "sick"
and "healthy" people. Explain how you strike this balance in your life.

Jesus answered them,
"Healthy people don't
need a doctor—sick
people do. I have come
to call sinners to turn
from their sins."

LUKE 5:31–32 NLT

What challenges stand in the way of your spending time among lost and broken people?

What can you do to overcome these challenges?

Write a prayer for the lost and broken people around you, expressing God's heart and desire that each of them turn to him.

<table>
<tr><td>DAY
30</td><td>Zacchaeus quickly climbed down and took Jesus to his house
in great excitement and joy. But the crowds were displeased.
"He has gone to be the guest of a notorious sinner," they grumbled.
LUKE 19:6–7 NLT</td></tr>
</table>

Today's Scripture Passage:

Reflections from my HEART:

I *Honor* who you are. (Praise God for something.)
I *Express* who I'm not. (Confess any known sin.)
I *Affirm* who I am in you. (How does God see you?)
I *Request* your will for me. (Ask God for something.)
I *Thank* you for what you've done. (Thank God for something.)

_____
_____
_____
_____
_____
_____
_____
_____
_____
_____
_____
_____
_____
_____
_____
_____

Today's Action Step:
_____
_____
_____
_____

30

As I grow in the Lord by reading his Word,
what am I learning from the life of Christ
(his identity, his personality, his priorities)?

How does he want me to live differently?

SURRENDERING TO CHRIST TOGETHER

WORSHIP

A life oriented toward worshipping God,
surrendering to him, begins with trust.

How easy or difficult is it for you to trust God? Explain your answer.

Do you agree with the statement, "True worship of God must begin with trust"?
Why or why not?

Jesus said to his
disciples, "Why are
you frightened?
Do you still have
no faith?"

MARK 4:40 TEV

What do you think about the statement, "Faith is not believing God can—faith is believing God will"?

In what areas are you having difficulty trusting God? How is Jesus challenging you to put your complete trust and faith in him?

DAY
31

O LORD, you answer us by giving us victory,
and you do wonderful things to save us.

PSALM 65:5 TEV

experiencing
CHRIST
together

Today's Scripture Passage:

Reflections from my HEART:

I *Honor* who you are. (Praise God for something.)
I *Express* who I'm not. (Confess any known sin.)
I *Affirm* who I am in you. (How does God see you?)
I *Request* your will for me. (Ask God for something.)
I *Thank* you for what you've done. (Thank God for something.)

DAY 31

_____
_____
_____
_____
_____
_____
_____
_____
_____
_____
_____
_____
_____
_____
_____
_____

Today's Action Step:

_____
_____
_____
_____

32

Often our goals conflict with God's agenda.
Then we have to decide, will I surrender my goal
or set aside God's agenda?

Surrendering our lives to the Lord is an important part of worship—
and where we will discover our greatest significance. How has surrender
played a role in your walk with God? How have you experienced significance
through these experiences?

What does it mean to you to "love your life down here on earth"?
What does it mean to "despise" it?

Jesus said, "If you love
your life down here—
you will lose it. If you
despise your life down
here—you will exchange
it for eternal glory."

JOHN 12:25 TLB

Jesus wants even our good earthly goals to be secondary to his agenda. Which of your goals have you surrendered to his will?

Which of your goals is the Lord still asking you to surrender?

What will it take, in a practical sense, for you to surrender these goals and dreams to Jesus?

> I consider everything a loss compared to the surpassing greatness of knowing Christ Jesus my Lord, for whose sake I have lost all things. I consider them rubbish, that I may gain Christ.
> **PHILIPPIANS 3:8**

DAY

32

_____

_____

_____

_____

_____

_____

_____

_____

_____

_____

_____

_____

_____

_____

_____

_____

_____

_____

experiencing
CHRIST
together

Today's Scripture Passage:

Reflections from my HEART:

I *Honor* who you are. (Praise God for something.)
I *Express* who I'm not. (Confess any known sin.)
I *Affirm* who I am in you. (How does God see you?)
I *Request* your will for me. (Ask God for something.)
I *Thank* you for what you've done. (Thank God for something.)

DAY
32

Today's Action Step:

33

God has called us to a "different kind" of greatness.

John the Baptist had status and esteem, but Jesus said that even the least person in God's kingdom is greater than he was. What does this statement mean to you?

Are there any areas in which you have been "great" in the world's eyes, but not as "great" in God's?

Are there any areas in which you've been "great" in God's eyes, but not in the world's?

Jesus said, "I tell you, of all who have ever lived, none is greater than John. Yet even the most insignificant person in the Kingdom of God is greater than he is!"

LUKE 7:28 NLT

John's attitude was that Jesus needed to become greater in his life, and his own desires, goals, and dreams should become less. To what desires, goals, and dreams in your own life do you need to apply this attitude?

Surrendering everything that you have and everything you hope to be can be a difficult thing to do. How can you make this surrender a form of worship to the Lord?

DAY 33

John the Baptist said, "He [Jesus] must become greater; I must become less."

JOHN 3:30

_____
_____
_____
_____
_____
_____
_____
_____
_____
_____
_____
_____
_____
_____
_____
_____
_____

experiencing CHRIST together

Today's Scripture Passage:

Reflections from my HEART:

I *Honor* who you are. (Praise God for something.)
I *Express* who I'm not. (Confess any known sin.)
I *Affirm* who I am in you. (How does God see you?)
I *Request* your will for me. (Ask God for something.)
I *Thank* you for what you've done. (Thank God for something.)

_____
_____
_____
_____
_____
_____
_____
_____
_____
_____
_____
_____
_____
_____
_____
_____

Today's Action Step:

_____
_____
_____
_____

34

JOURNAL DAY 34

When we grasp who Jesus is and what he does for us,
we aren't just grateful in words.
We respond with full surrender of our lives.

Jesus died on the cross for our sins, but most of us don't keep that in our minds from day to day. What can you do to maintain a fresh sense of gratitude for his sacrifice?

In addition to the cross, what has Jesus done that deserves extravagant love, gratitude, or worship from you? How can you begin to praise him for the things he has done?

Jesus said, "You did not put oil on my head, but she has poured perfume on my feet. Therefore, I tell you, her many sins have been forgiven—for she loved much. But he who has been forgiven little loves little."

LUKE 7:46–47

For what things in your life are you the most thankful?

For what things are you the least thankful? What would it take for you to move these things from the "least thankful" to the "most thankful" category?

Opening your heart and expressing your thanks to God is an intimate act of worship. Write a prayer of worship to God, telling him of your deep gratitude for the things that he has done.

Continue to live in Christ Jesus, ... overflowing with thankfulness.

COLOSSIANS 2:6–7

DAY
34

Today's Scripture Passage:

Reflections from my HEART:

I *Honor* who you are. (Praise God for something.)
I *Express* who I'm not. (Confess any known sin.)
I *Affirm* who I am in you. (How does God see you?)
I *Request* your will for me. (Ask God for something.)
I *Thank* you for what you've done. (Thank God for something.)

DAY
34

Today's Action Step:

35

There are times when doing the right thing means venturing into the unknown, when doing God's will is costly. At those times, knowing Jesus has been there ahead of us can make a huge difference.

Surrendering to the Father was not always easy for Jesus, especially when he was facing the cross. What does this mean to you when you are facing difficult choices in your life?

Ecclesiastes 7:3 says that sorrow can be better than laughter. Has there ever been a time when this was the case for you? What was the situation? What was the end result?

Let us fix our eyes on Jesus, the author and perfecter of our faith, who for the joy set before him endured the cross.

HEBREWS 12:2

Passive surrender is acceptance of what is—an illness, a job loss, a crisis with our children. Active surrender is the decision to take action in accord with what we believe God wants us to do.

What areas of your life have you passively surrendered to the Lord? What was the result? Which areas do you still need to accept?

What areas of your life have you actively surrendered to the Lord? What was the result? How do you need to continue actively surrendering your life to him?

DAY 35

Sorrow is better than laughter, for sadness has a refining influence on us.

ECCLESIASTES 7:3 NLT

_____

_____

_____

_____

_____

_____

_____

_____

_____

_____

_____

_____

_____

_____

_____

_____

_____

experiencing CHRIST together

Today's Scripture Passage:

Reflections from my HEART:

I *Honor* who you are. (Praise God for something.)
I *Express* who I'm not. (Confess any known sin.)
I *Affirm* who I am in you. (How does God see you?)
I *Request* your will for me. (Ask God for something.)
I *Thank* you for what you've done. (Thank God for something.)

DAY 35

_____
_____
_____
_____
_____
_____
_____
_____
_____
_____
_____
_____
_____
_____
_____
_____
_____

Today's Action Step:

_____
_____
_____
_____

36

If we want to live with perseverance and joy rather than drivenness and despair, we have only to look into the eyes of the Lord who triumphed over death.

How has Jesus' resurrection affected you on a personal, emotional level?

How has the resurrection affected the way you live your life—the choices you have made?

The angel said to the women, ... "Jesus, who was crucified, ... is not here; he has risen, just as he said."

MATTHEW 28:5–6

Jesus' resurrection gives us the power to live a new life, starting now. What will your new life look like? How will it be different from the life you have been living?

Take a few moments and consider your life at this moment—what it is and what you want it to be. Write out the words, "Here I am, Lord. Use me." Then write down whatever you feel God wants you to do with the rest of your life. Finally, write a statement of commitment to follow him wherever he leads.

> Just as Christ was raised from the dead through the glory of the Father, we too may live a new life.
>
> **ROMANS 6:4**

DAY
36

Today's Scripture Passage:

Reflections from my HEART:

I *Honor* who you are. (Praise God for something.)
I *Express* who I'm not. (Confess any known sin.)
I *Affirm* who I am in you. (How does God see you?)
I *Request* your will for me. (Ask God for something.)
I *Thank* you for what you've done. (Thank God for something.)

DAY
36

Today's Action Step:

As I grow in the Lord by reading his Word,
what am I learning from the life of Christ
(his identity, his personality, his priorities)?

36

How does he want me to live differently?

36

As I have grown in the Lord by reading his Word throughout the last few months, what have I learned from the life of Christ (his identity, his personality, his priorities)?

_____

_____

_____

_____

_____

_____

_____

_____

_____

_____

_____

_____

_____

_____

_____

_____

_____

_____

_____

_____

How have I begun to live my life differently?
How can I continue to live my life differently in the future?

NEW TESTAMENT
READING PLAN

PURPOSE-DRIVEN LIFE HEALTH ASSESSMENT

	Just Beginning	Getting Going	Well Developed

CONNECTING WITH GOD'S FAMILY

I am deepening my understanding of and friendship with God in community with others	1	2	3	4	5
I am growing in my ability both to share and to show my love to others	1	2	3	4	5
I am willing to share my real needs for prayer and support from others	1	2	3	4	5
I am resolving conflict constructively and am willing to forgive others	1	2	3	4	5

CONNECTING Total _____

GROWING TO BE LIKE CHRIST

I have a growing relationship with God through regular time in the Bible and in prayer (spiritual habits)	1	2	3	4	5
I am experiencing more of the characteristics of Jesus Christ (love, joy, peace, patience, kindness, self-control, etc.) in my life	1	2	3	4	5
I am avoiding addictive behaviors (food, television, busyness, and the like) to meet my needs	1	2	3	4	5
I am spending time with a Christian friend (spiritual partner) who celebrates and challenges my spiritual growth	1	2	3	4	5

GROWING Total _____

DEVELOPING YOUR SHAPE TO SERVE OTHERS

I have discovered and am further developing my unique God-given shape for ministry	1	2	3	4	5
I am regularly praying for God to show me opportunities to serve him and others	1	2	3	4	5
I am serving in a regular (once a month or more) ministry in the church or community	1	2	3	4	5
I am a team player in my small group by sharing some group role or responsibility	1	2	3	4	5

DEVELOPING Total_____

SHARING YOUR LIFE MISSION EVERY DAY

I am cultivating relationships with non-Christians and praying
    for God to give me natural opportunities to share his love   1 2 3 4 5

I am investing my time in another person or group who needs
    to know Christ personally   1 2 3 4 5

I am regularly inviting unchurched or unconnected friends to
    my church or small group   1 2 3 4 5

I am praying and learning about where God can use me and
    our group cross-culturally for missions   1 2 3 4 5

SHARING Total _____

SURRENDERING YOUR LIFE FOR GOD'S PLEASURE

I am experiencing more of the presence and power of God in
    my everyday life   1 2 3 4 5

I am faithfully attending my small group and weekend services
    to worship God   1 2 3 4 5

I am seeking to please God by surrendering every area of my life
    (health, decisions, finances, relationships, future, etc.) to him   1 2 3 4 5

I am accepting the things I cannot change and becoming
    increasingly grateful for the life I've been given   1 2 3 4 5

SURRENDERING Total_____

Total your scores for each purpose, and place them on the chart below. Reassess
your progress at the end of thirty days. Be sure to select your spiritual partner and
the one area in which you'd like to make progress over the next thirty days.

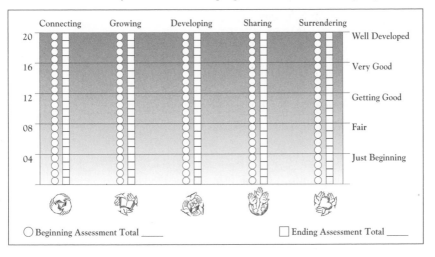

PURPOSE-DRIVEN LIFE HEALTH PLAN

My Name _____ Date _____

My Spiritual Partner _____ Date _____

Possibilities	Plan
	(make one goal for each area)

CONNECTING WITH GOD'S FAMILY
Hebrews 10:24 – 25; Ephesians 2:19
How can I deepen my relationships with others?

- Attend my group more faithfully

- Schedule lunch with a group member

- Begin praying for a spiritual mentor

WHO is/are my shepherd(s)?

NAME: _____

GROWING TO BE LIKE CHRIST
Colossians 1:28; Ephesians 4:15
How can I grow to be like Christ?

- Commit to personal time with God three days a week

- Ask a friend for devotional accountability

- Begin journaling my prayers

WHAT is my Spiritual Health Plan?

RENEWAL DATE: _____

DEVELOPING YOUR SHAPE TO SERVE OTHERS
Ephesians 4:11 – 13; 1 Corinthians 12:7; 1 Peter 3:10
How can I develop my shape for ministry?

- Begin praying for a personal ministry

- Attend a gift discovery class

- Serve together at a church event or in the community

WHERE am I serving others?

MINISTRY: _____

SHARING YOUR LIFE MISSION EVERY DAY
Matthew 28:18 – 20; Acts 20:24
How can I share my faith every day?

- Start meeting for lunch with a seeker friend

- Invite a non-Christian relative to church

- Pray for and support an overseas missionary

WHEN am I sharing my life mission?

TIME: _____

SURRENDERING YOUR LIFE FOR GOD'S PLEASURE
How can I surrender my life for God's pleasure?

- Submit one area to God

- Be honest about my struggle and hurt

- Buy a music CD for worship in my car and in the group

HOW am I surrendering my life today?

AREA: _____

SHAPE
WORKSHEET

God has designed you with a unique SHAPE. Your SHAPE enables you to serve God in ways no other person can. It makes you irreplaceable. If you know your SHAPE, you'll have many clues about the service to which God is calling you. Discerning God's will for your life becomes much easier.

This worksheet will help you discover and develop your SHAPE. By the end of session 6, you will have all five areas filled out. You will also have feedback from your group members that affirms what they see in you for each area. Use this worksheet as a guideline for choosing ministry both inside and outside your group.

S*piritual Gifts*

- [ ] Preaching
- [ ] Evangelism
- [ ] Discernment
- [ ] Apostle
- [ ] Teaching
- [ ] Encouragement
- [ ] Wisdom
- [ ] Missions
- [ ] Service
- [ ] Mercy
- [ ] Hospitality
- [ ] Pastoring
- [ ] Giving
- [ ] Intercession
- [ ] Music
- [ ] Arts and Crafts
- [ ] Healing
- [ ] Miracles
- [ ] Leadership
- [ ] Administration
- [ ] Faith

H*eart — I Love to*

- [ ] design/develop
- [ ] pioneer
- [ ] organize
- [ ] operate/maintain
- [ ] serve/help
- [ ] acquire/possess
- [ ] excel
- [ ] perform
- [ ] improve
- [ ] repair
- [ ] lead/be in charge
- [ ] persevere
- [ ] follow the rules
- [ ] prevail
- [ ] influence

Abilities

- [ ] Entertaining
- [ ] Recruiting
- [ ] Interviewing
- [ ] Researching
- [ ] Artistic/Graphics
- [ ] Evaluating
- [ ] Planning
- [ ] Managing
- [ ] Counseling
- [ ] Teaching
- [ ] Writing/Editing
- [ ] Promoting
- [ ] Repairing
- [ ] Feeding
- [ ] Recall
- [ ] Mechanical Operating
- [ ] Resourceful
- [ ] Counting/Classifying
- [ ] Public Relations
- [ ] Welcoming
- [ ] Composing
- [ ] Landscaping
- [ ] Arts and Crafts
- [ ] Decorating
- [ ] Musical
- [ ] Other _____
- [ ] Other _____

Experiences

- [ ] Spiritual:

- [ ] Painful:

- [ ] Education:

- [ ] Work:

- [ ] Ministry:

Personality

	Hi	Lo	Lo	Hi	
Introverted	[ ]	[ ]	[ ]	[ ]	Extroverted
Variety	[ ]	[ ]	[ ]	[ ]	Routine
Self-Expressive	[ ]	[ ]	[ ]	[ ]	Self-Controlled
Competitive	[ ]	[ ]	[ ]	[ ]	Cooperative

KEY VERSES
TO MEMORIZE

Matthew 5:8	2 Timothy 1:6
Ephesians 4:32	Genesis 50:20
Proverbs 27:17	Matthew 19:26
James 5:16	John 3:16
Proverbs 25:11	Luke 19:10
Psalm 9:1	2 Corinthians 5:20
Matthew 6:33	Colossians 4:5
Ephesians 3:16–17	2 Peter 3:9
Luke 10:41–42	Matthew 28:19–20
Psalm 46:10	Romans 12:1
2 Timothy 2:15	Psalm 145:3
James 1:2–3	Psalm 139:16
Psalm 139:14	Hebrews 11:6
Mark 10:43	Philippians 3:7
1 Peter 4:10	Psalm 31:5

At Inspirio we love to hear from you—your
stories, your feedback,
and your product ideas.
Please send your comments to us
by way of email at
icares@zondervan.com
or to the address below:

inspirio

Attn: Inspirio Cares
5300 Patterson Avenue SE
Grand Rapids, MI 49530

If you would like further information
about Inspirio and the products we
create please visit us at:
www.inspiriogifts.com

Thank you and God bless!